MW00387595

# MINSTROLOGY
## A MINSTREL TRAINING BOOKLET

# PAUL ANDERSON

Printed in the United States of America First Printing, 2019

ISBN 9781796293500


Cover design done by: Damascus Media

Formatting and Diagrams done by: Tymeless Forms

# DEDICATION POEM

Stay your hand young David

Stay your hand

Strike the lyre young minstrel

Play the band

Something's stirring son of Jesse

Something's stirring

Hearts are burning

Elisha's servant

Tides are turning

Make war you sons of Asaph, Haman, and

Jeduthan

For The battle is The Lord's

Release your sword

And the people of God will go forth.

Raise your sound and the walls will come down

Minstrel, Minstrel the time is now

Stir up the atmosphere with your cymbals and

synths, the bass, the keys, organ,


and RIFF!

There's a shaking in the spirit

Play the VI!

Here comes the shift!

Now ride the wave

Stay you hand young David,

this is your day!

# MINSTROLOGY:

# A Minstrel Training Booklet

# CONTENTS

# INTRODUCTION

Often times, when God wants to do something new in an individual, He will change his/her name to better fit the description of their assignment. He changed his disciples who were fishermen to fishers of men, from Abram to Abraham, from Simon to Cephas.

*Nagawn.* The Hebrew translation of where we get the word *Minstrel.* This word is interchangeable with *musician*, or *string player.* However, we will use the word Minstrel to create distinction between one who plays for entertainment and who plays for the glory of God.

This booklet contains principles and tools that can be applied to any musician; no matter the skill level. Why? Because the difference between a musician and a minstrel is not how well they can manipulate their instrument but how well they manipulate the heavens! I believe God has given me a mandate to revive and re-establish the office of the minstrel in the 21$^{st}$ century church! To 9restore honor to those gifts that release atmospheres of worship in the house of The Lord. To activate musicians into minstrels that prophesy The Word and are true worshippers of God.

Back in 2010, I met my Spiritual father, Apostle Bryan Meadows who gave me an apostolic assignment to raise up minstrels. Not soon after I began to see that there was MORE. What do I mean by more? Before, I thought that playing in church just included learning your music, shedding, and putting together a performance that would entertain the people of God. But then I realized The Lord wanted to use us (musicians) for more! I came to the revelation of our prophetic significance! That through Christ, we can prophesy, cast out devils, shift atmospheres and create waves of glory for God to dwell in! Believe me, once you experience the higher calling of your gift, you won't be satisfied with normal musicianship! This generation is crying out for a sound, will you answer?

# KEYS

**The Art of Warfare** (Key Scriptures: Psalm 91:1; 2 Samuel 1:18, 2 Chronicles 2:20)

One of the main weapons that the church possesses is the ability to war and take authority in the unseen world also known as "the spirit realm". Minstrels play a major role in this activity. HOW?

Because there are many instances in The Word where God used A MIGHTY SOUND or THE SOUND OF WORSHIP to defeat the enemies of his people, Israel.

In 2 Chronicles 20, the Israelites were faced against a great army that were coming to attack them, but instead of fighting, they released the Levites (aka the Minstrels) to sing of the goodness of The Lord and it CONFUSED THE ENEMY!

*Now when they began to sing and to praise, the LORD set ambushes against the people of Ammon, Moab, and Mount Seir, who had come against Judah; and they were defeated. ²³ For the people of Ammon and Moab stood up against the inhabitants of Mount Seir to utterly kill and destroy them. And when they [e] had made an end of the inhabitants of Seir, they helped to destroy one another.*

*²⁴ So when Judah came to a place overlooking the wilderness, they looked toward the multitude; and there were their dead bodies, fallen on the earth. No one had escaped.*

As you can see, we wrestle NOT against flesh and blood but against principalities, against powers. Our warfare is not physical but spiritual and "is not by power or by might, but by His Spirit" that we conquer the enemy!

With that being said, **the key to Art of Warfare is WORSHIP**! We access our authority and power through communion and fellowship with Jesus and as we exalt Him, in this case on our instrument, with our song, you will began to see a release of power that overthrows every enemy you face. King

David understood this principle as a minstrel and a warrior. In 2 Samuel 1:18, he commanded that the children of Judah be taught "The song of the Bow". This was a song of lament over the death of Saul and Johnathan. However we know from the Psalms that David had a way of taking his worries and turning it into worship. The song of the bow was a song that was played upon a bowed instrument, one with strings, similar to his instrument of warfare, the bow and arrow. He wrote in Psalm 144:1, "Blessed be the Lord my rock who trains my **hands for war** and my fingers for battle." **The Lord taught him how to fight through his worship!** The quickness used to pluck his strings on the harp, helped him to quickly fire at his enemies with the bow and arrow!

You see, a minstrel's worship is dangerous to the enemy because as they worship, their hands become WEAPONS! Minstrels, as you worship your hands will began to open the heavens and the devil will be reminded of every battle that was lost at the hand of a minstrel!

# Challenge #1

Being a minstrel is about operating in skill and anointing. Skill is attained through study and practice. Anointing comes in communion with the Holy Spirit and through consecration.

Take 10 days to listen and seek the sound of heaven. Consecrate your ears! No music for 10 days! This is a "music fast"!

During that time, sing to The Lord and listen for a new sound.

## Notes Section:

**Creating One Sound** (Key Scripture: 1 Chronicles 5:13)

In 2 chronicles 5:13, during the dedication of Solomon's temple in Israel, something significant happened. **"...the house of The Lord, was filled with a cloud, so that the priests could not stand to minister because of the cloud, for the GLORY of The Lord filled the house of God.**

As minstrels, this is our goal! We are anointed to release a sound that will lead people to a place of worship, so that the glory of God would manifest. But how? What is that sound? We can't go back in time and hear the exact chords and rhythms, but we can study the Word to find the key that unlocks Heaven's door!

The key is **One Sound**! In the beginning of that verse, it says that "...when the trumpeters and singers were **as one**, **to make one sound** to be heard in praising and thanking The Lord..." As you can see, it isn't about WHAT you play, but WHY you play and HOW you play it! Heaven doesn't necessarily respond to a certain chord but to a sound of AGREEMENT! Agreement is a spiritual technology that the Heavens cannot ignore! That's why Jesus said, "Again I say unto you, that if two of you shall **agree** on earth as touching ANYTHING that they shall ask, it shall be done for them of my Father which is in heaven." (Matthew 18:19) However, in order to make one sound you don't have to have the same sound, but you create one sound through LAYERS. Line upon line, precept upon precept (Isaiah 28:10), and these layers agree AS ONE! So, to create one sound, you actually NEED different sounds, from the organ to guitar, to voices, to cymbals. From CCM to Gospel, from Reggae to EDM/Dance music. When any of these come together and agree on praising God, we will see heaven respond WITH GLORY!

## Challenge #2

Take a scripture, read it, pray, and ask for God's heart concerning that verse. As a minstrel you are not able to speak words but you can articulate the <u>emotion behind the scripture</u>. Doing this helps create a relationship between your gift and The Word of God. When God speaks He releases more than words, but a burden or feeling that sometimes can only be articulated through a sound! Do this every day for a week!

## Notes Section:

**Flowing in the Prophetic** (2 Kings 3:15)

The problem we see today when it comes to worship in the church is the emphasis on the CREATION rather than that CREATOR. While musicians are to play skillfully, their skills must not supersede their **assignment** in worship. The assignment is His presence, and our purpose is to unify the hearts and minds of people through song, through a sound that gives glory to Him. This is where it all starts; **Minstrels produce a sound that intentionally puts the attention on God!** If out of the abundance of the heart the mouth speaks, then out the abundance of the heart, the minstrel plays. It is the desire of every minstrel, because he/she is a worshipper, to release a sound that activates "the hand of Lord". Which brings us to our key scripture, in 2 Kings 3:15, the prophet Elisha was approached by three kings seeking prophetic counsel concerning an enemy nation that they were going to war with. However, there was strife in that meeting because the King of Israel at that time did not serve the God of Elisha, but worshipped false gods. For Elisha said,

*"...surely were it not I regarded the presence of Jehoshaphat king of Judah, I would not look at you nor see you. But now bring me a minstrel..."* (v. 14,15)

Wow! Imagine this moment, the atmosphere wasn't necessarily conducive for prophetic ministry. However, at that moment, the fate of three kingdoms rested in the hands a minstrel. He would shift the atmosphere by releasing a sound that would activate the hand of Lord.

*"...when the minstrel played, the hand of The Lord came upon him." (v.15)*

Minstrels are wired to discern atmospheres and with a sensitive spirit and skilled hands, they usher in His Presence for a purpose greater than them! My question to you is, what is the purpose of the sound you are releasing? Who do you intend to glorify? Always asking and answering these questions while ministering will help you maintain the right perspective and keep you focused.

## Notes Section:

# Part. 2

Playing prophetically is about playing with discernment, but it is also about playing with understanding, and that of His Word! Why? I will give you two words: **Minstrels Prophesy!**

The word prophecy in scripture can be translated into the word *"propheteo"* and it means to speak from inspiration. **Minstrels prophesy when they play from inspiration of God's word**. This can be through worship, a prophetic atmosphere, or by hearing or reading the Word of God.

 For example:

In John 3 Jesus explains to Nicodemus that the Spirit of God is like the wind. As a minstrel I can articulate that scripture through cymbal rolls and wind chimes, or by playing a wind instrument that carries an airy sound.

The goal is to have a relationship with The Word in such a way, that you are able to relay the message of the text through music!

Here is a list of <u>atmospheres/sounds</u> that Minstrels can articulate, how do I know? Because I've heard it and experienced it. While this list is not comprehensive, it can increase your expectation with what The Lord desires to do through you next time you play:

- **The Judgement of God**
- **The Fire of God**
- **The Mysteries of God**
- **The Wind of God**
- **The Heart of God**
- **The Rivers of God**
- **The Peace of God**

## Challenge #3

Everyday we are faced with the issues of life. However, it is our response to those issues that determines whether we live in victory or defeat. I challenge you to do is David did. Take your worries, problems, issues and begin to worship God OVER them! In 1 Samuel 16 David was able to refresh Saul and pull him out of his distress. He was only able this because he had done so for years through his own personal worship.

## Notes Section:

_____

_____

_____

_____

_____

_____

_____

_____

_____

_____

_____

_____

_____

_____

*Playing with Purpose* *(1 Corinthians 14:7-8)*

A Sound is produced through purpose. Ask yourself, what is your purpose for playing your instrument? Why do you play?
Because your purpose will be your desire!

In 1 Corinthians 14:7-8 Paul compares speaking in tongues without interpretation like a trumpet that makes an "uncertain sound".

"And even things without life giving sound, whether pipe or harp, except they give a distinction in the sounds, how shall it be known what is piped or harped? For if the trumpet gives an uncertain sound, who shall prepare himself to the battle?"
1 Corinthians 14:7-8 KJV

A sound is characterized by its intention and can be confirmed by its response. In other words, does the sound you produce cause the hearers to worship God or worship your gift? What is the response your looking for? That will be determined by your intention when you approach your instrument. The desire of the Minstrel is always to release a sound that activates faith in the believer; it's an anointed sound that can be distinguished not only with the ears but with heart and the spirit!

That's also why it's important for Minstrels to know and Love the Word of God. Because if you do not agree with the words and songs that are being lifted up in worship, you will inevitably produce a sound that is unfruitful. Which could in turn produce what the scripture calls STRANGE FIRE!

**Musicians BEWARE:**

The ministry unto God and His people is sacred! Too many musicians treat playing in church like any other gig, which can produce "strange fire" and can get you in a lot of trouble with God.

**What is Strange Fire?**

According to Leviticus 10:1, Aaron's sons, Nadab and Abihu, were ministering before the Lord in the tabernacle and had created incense (fire) in a way that God had not instructed them to. In other words, they had become familiar or common with God and His Presence and began to treat His tabernacle without the respect it deserves. Therefore, they offered to God an unholy sacrifice that resulted in their demise.

"Aaron's sons Nadab and Abihu took their censers, put fire in them and added incense; and they offered unauthorized fire before the LORD, contrary to his command. And there went out fire from the Lord, and devoured them, and they died before the Lord." Leviticus 10:2 KJV

Playing with purpose is all about being connected to what God wants to do through us and through His people. Our sound is established through our purpose. When we connect our purpose with His, and submit our desires to His, the sound of heaven is released, and WE BECOME THE INSTRUMENTS.

## Notes section:

# Scriptures:

## *1 Corinthians 14:7-8*

*Even in the case of lifeless things that make sounds, such as the pipe or harp, how will anyone know what tune is being played unless there is a distinction in the notes? Again, if the trumpet does not sound a clear call, who will get ready for battle?*

## Psalms 144:1

*Praise be to the LORD my Rock, who trains my hands for war, my fingers for battle.*

## 2 Kings 3:15

*But now bring me a minstrel. And it came to pass, when the minstrel played, that the hand of the LORD came upon him.*

**Psalm 57:8**

*Awake up, my glory; awake, psaltery and harp: I myself will awaken the dawn.*

**Isaiah 30:32**

*And in every place where the grounded staff shall pass, which the LORD shall lay upon him, it shall be with tabrets and harps: and in battles of shaking will he fight with it.*

**1 Chronicles 25:2**

*Of the sons of Asaph; Zaccur, and Joseph, and Nethaniah, and Asarelah, the sons of Asaph under the hands of Asaph, which prophesied according to the order of the king.*

**Zephaniah 3:17**

*The L*ORD* your God is with you, the Mighty Warrior who saves. He will take great delight in you; in his love he will no longer rebuke you,* **but will rejoice over you with singing.**

*2 Chronicles 5:13*

*Indeed it came to pass, when the trumpeters and singers were as one, to make one sound to be heard in praising and thanking the Lord, and when they lifted up their voice with the trumpets and cymbals and instruments of music, and praised the Lord, saying: "For He is good, For His mercy endures forever," that the house, the house of the Lord, was filled with a cloud,"*

# DECLARATIONS

## PROPHETIC DECLARATIONS

These declarations will activate the minstrel anointing in you! These activation statements are meant to not only build your faith but create a vision of your purpose and destiny. Your spirit-man responds to the word of God being spoken (Romans 10:17). These declarations were given to me one day as I watching television and God spoke to me and told me write them down and speak them over myself and band before we ministered. After releasing these declarations, we all felt a shift in our approach to our assignment and a greater faith to walk in the anointing of the minstrel.

**Step 1:**

Read these declarations aloud with your team or by yourself before your minister

**Step 2:**

As you read, begin to visualize yourself doing what it you are saying!

**Step 3:**

RECEIVE! RECEIVE! RECEIVE! Begin to play what you hear and feel in your heart or spirit, and flow in the anointing that was just activated in you!

# NOW LET'S

# DECLARE

# THESE THINGS!

## DECLARATIONS:

1. I AM A MINSTREL OF GOD (I AM GOD'S MINSTREL)

2. I CAST OUT DEVILS WHEN I PLAY MY INSTRUMENT

3. I OPEN HEAVEN WHEN I PLAY AND WORSHIP ON MY INSTRUMENT

4. WHEN I PLAY MY INSTRUMENT, I GIVE GLORY TO GOD

5. I PLAY UNDER THE ANOINTING OF GOD

6. I HAVE BEEN ANOINTED TO SHIFT ATMOSPHERES

7. I PROPHESY THROUGH MY INSTRUMENT

8. I PROPHESY ACCORDING THE ORDER OF THE KING – JESUS

9. I AM CONFIDENT IN MY GOD-GIVEN GIFT, AND I BIND DISCOURAGEMENT IN JESUS NAME

10. WHEN I PLAY, I CREATE A SOUND THAT SHAKES THE HEAVENS AND ACTIVATES THE HAND OF LORD.

# DIAGRAMS

# DIAGRAMS

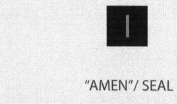

"AMEN"/ SEAL

**(I) Amen/The Seal:** The (I) chord is the first chord in the scale, however it is the often the last chord to be sustained in prophetic moments because it SEALS the moment. It seals a decree, a deliverance or a message and it is also known as the "amen" or "it is so" chord. This chord is a judgment chord. When The Lord is releasing judgment upon a situation, this chord releases a sound of agreement with what was released. You might also play V-I to accent this chord and give it more dominance.

# DIAGRAMS

## RETRACT/EXPAND

**(IV) Open the Heavens:** The IV chord is sometimes seen is as a "worship" chord. This chord causes the heavens to **retract or expand**. In this diagram it is shaped as an outward V. That's because this chord actually opens heavens by releasing a sound that encourages us to receive. Heaven opens when we receive and submit. It's a sound of intentional surrender or Selah!

This sound is also a **sound of unity**! This is prophetic because, you will notice that the (IV) chord is the only chord that can hold any note in the scale without sounding dissonant. As I mentioned in the creating one sound section, unity and agreement is a technology that heaven cannot ignore, so when you play this chord, expect for hearts and minds to unify to what God is doing!

# DIAGRAMS

## STANDSTILL/ATTENTION

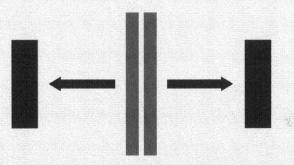

**(V) Praise/Expectancy:** The (V) chord demonstrates a sound of suspended praise and expectation! This chord releases a sound that causes hearts and the heavens to SWING OPEN AND STAY OPEN. In music theory it is the called the "dominant". The dominant chord is like the hinge upon which every other note in scale hangs upon. So this chord is like the beginning or the doorway to a SHIFT! **Play this chord if the atmosphere needs to shift to a standstill or to stand at "attention".**

# DIAGRAMS

## ADVANCE/PROTRACT

**(vi) Advance the Heavens:** The (VI) chord is pointed outward because it is the sound that advances the heavens and causes the heavens to protract by applying pressure. This chord puts a demand on heaven and on an atmosphere to be <u>shaken up</u>. It is a minor chord that carries an aggressive sound and causes a major shift! This chord can be used for **warfare, deliverance, strong intercession, mysteries, travailing, and repentance.**

# PRAYER

Father, I thank you for every minstrel that you are raising up in this generation and the generations to come. I pray for everyone that reads this book, that they would be empowered to walk in their purpose as a minstrel. I decree and declare that fear is breaking off of their lives as they accept their calling. Father, let the spirit of religion be broken off of their gift as they prepare to flow in fresh streams of worship. I pray that they would release the hand of The Lord when they play according to 2 Kings 3:15, I pray that they would experience the same atmospheres they create for others. I pray that they may prophesy through their instrument and that they would use their sound to make war against the kingdom of darkness. I declare that their hands are weapons and that according to Psalm 144:1, The Lord would teach their hands to war and their fingers to fight in Jesus name, amen.

# STUDY QUESTIONS

**1. What are some ways that you could articulate/prophesy what God is doing in a service? Think creatively and take time to be inspired by the Holy Spirit.**

_____

_____

_____

_____

_____

_____

_____

_____

_____

_____

_____

_____

_____

_____

**2. Agreement is a technology of the kingdom. How can you create unity in your team both on and off of your instrument?**

_____

_____

_____

_____

_____

_____

_____

_____

_____

_____

_____

_____

_____

_____

**3. Have you ever seen or experienced God use music, through you or through someone else, to release true breakthrough, healing or miracles? What was the atmosphere like? How can you create or sustain that atmosphere in your house of worship?**

_____

_____

_____

_____

_____

_____

_____

_____

_____

_____

_____

4. Now that you've read this book how will you approach your instrument or your ministry as a minstrel differently?

_____

_____

_____

_____

_____

_____

_____

_____

_____

_____

_____

_____

5. David is a prime example of a minstrel that we have to learn from. God used him mightily through his gift. But it did not come without a price! Study 1 Samuel 16. What was the process and his lifestyle like that qualified him for the anointing?

_____

_____

_____

_____

_____

_____

_____

_____

_____

_____

_____

_____

6. In 1 Chronicles 25 David is setting up the tabernacle. In doing so, he splits up the musicians into three different groups and gave each of them an assignment. What were those groups? How did they serve to help enhance worship in God's house?

_____

_____

_____

_____

_____

_____

_____

_____

_____

_____

7. In the "keys" section, we learned about "strange fire" in Leviticus 10. What are some ways that you can keep your heart and ministry pure before The Lord?

_____

_____

_____

_____

_____

_____

_____

_____

_____

_____

_____

_____

_____

# JOURNAL

*"Even in the case of lifeless things that make sounds, such as the pipe or harp, how will anyone know what tune is being played unless there is a distinction in the notes? Again, if the trumpet does not sound a clear call, who will get ready for battle?"* **1 Corinthians 14:7-8**

_____

_____

_____

_____

_____

_____

_____

_____

_____

_____

_____

_____

_____

_____

_____

_____

_____

_____

_____

_____

_____

*"Praise be to the LORD my Rock, who trains my hands for war, my fingers for battle."* **Psalms 144:1**

_____

_____

_____

_____

_____

_____

_____

_____

_____

_____

_____

_____

_____

_____

_____

_____

_____

_____

_____

_____

_____

_____

_____

*"But now bring me a minstrel. And it came to pass, when the minstrel played, that the hand of the LORD came upon him."*
**2 Kings 3:15**

_____

_____

_____

_____

_____

_____

_____

_____

_____

_____

_____

_____

_____

_____

_____

_____

_____

_____

_____

_____

_____

_____

_____

*"Awake up, my glory; awake, psaltery and harp: I myself will awaken the dawn."* **Psalm 57:8**

_____
_____
_____
_____
_____
_____
_____
_____
_____
_____
_____
_____
_____
_____
_____
_____
_____
_____
_____
_____
_____
_____
_____

*"And in every place where the grounded staff shall pass, which the LORD shall lay upon him, it shall be with tabrets and harps: and in battles of shaking will he fight with it."*  **Isaiah 30:32**

*"Indeed it came to pass, when the trumpeters and singers were as one, to make one sound to be heard in praising and thanking the Lord, and when they lifted up their voice with the trumpets and cymbals and instruments of music, and praised the Lord, saying: "For He is good, For His mercy endures forever," that the house, the house of the Lord, was filled with a cloud,"* **2 Chronicles 5:13**

_____

_____

_____

_____

_____

_____

_____

_____

_____

_____

_____

_____

_____

_____

_____

_____

_____

_____

_____

_____

*"The LORD your God is with you, the Mighty Warrior who saves. He will take great delight in you; in his love he will no longer rebuke you, but will rejoice over you with singing."* **Zephaniah 3:17**

"Aaron's sons Nadab and Abihu took their censers, put fire in them and added incense; and they offered unauthorized fire before the LORD, contrary to his command. And there went out fire from the Lord, and devoured them, and they died before the Lord."
**Leviticus 10:2 KJV**

*"and he ordered that the people of Judah be taught this lament of the bow (it is written in the Book of Jasher): NIV* **2 Samuel 1:18**

_____

_____

_____

_____

_____

_____

_____

_____

_____

_____

_____

_____

_____

_____

_____

_____

_____

_____

_____

_____

_____

_____

_____

_____

_____

_____

_____

_____

_____

*Of the sons of Asaph; Zaccur, and Joseph, and Nethaniah, and Asarelah, the sons of Asaph under the hands of Asaph, which prophesied according to the order of the king."*
**1 Chronicles 25:2**

_____

_____

_____

_____

_____

_____

_____

_____

_____

_____

_____

_____

_____

_____

_____

_____

_____

_____

_____

_____

_____

_____

Made in the USA
Columbia, SC
10 March 2019